It's Everybody's World

We either Live Together or Die Together

Robin Arthur

En Route Books and Media, LLC
St. Louis, MO, USA

Make the time

Enroute Books and Media, LLC
5705 Rhodes Avenue
St Louis, MO, 63109

Cover Design: Aaron Arthur from photo by Anna Shvets
https://www.pexels.com/photo/earth-globe-with-googly-eyes-on-gray-background-5217882/

ISBN: 979-8-88870-182-9 and 979-8-88870-186-7
Library of Congress Control Number: 2024938053

Copyright © 2024 Robin Arthur

All rights reserved. No part of this book may be reproduced, stored in a retrieval system, or transmitted in any form, or by any means, electronic, mechanical, photocopying or otherwise, without the prior written permission of the author.

Table of Contents

Preface iii

PART I: A Prelude 1
   Another World Somewhere 3

PART II: Think Globally 25

   Chapter 1: The Troubles with Nationalism. A Distasteful Déjà Vu 27
   Chapter 2: Globalisation is not optional. We either live together or die together. 37
   Chapter 3: Migration is a Catalyst 41
   Chapter 4: Religious Diversity is a Boon, not a Threat 49
   Chapter 5: Literacy is Key to its Success 67
   Chapter 6: Refugees are Part of our Globalised World 75

PART III: Create a world with a heart of gold. 81

   Story 1: Holocaust survivor tells of the burning of Jews at the crematoriums 83

Story 2: Mary tells of Chinese people pictured in cartoons eating rats............87

Story 3: Canadian patient screams at the sight of Nigerian doctor............91

Story 4: Cambodian baby flown to Canada in the heat of the war............97

Story 5: Kosovar doctor recalls the nightmare of war 101

Story 6: Vietnamese chooses dangerous sea ordeal to flee............ 105

Story 7: Somalian hopes Canada will erase those horror memories............ 109

Story 8: Journalist once hobnobbing with Saddam Hussein flees Iraq............ 111

Story 9: Kurdish farmer escapes Iraq's chemical poisoning. 115

Epilogue............ 119

References 121

Preface

The evolution of man has taken *sapiens* from what was apparently a world in the wilderness back in the day to a state of intellectual excellence. The progress of mankind has been swift and stunning. The twentieth century may have transported man's comprehension of the universe to new heights and his understanding of the scientific world to new horizons. But it also demonstrated in two bloody wars in the first half of that century, man's senseless desire - inspired by hate - to capture and seize, to dehumanise and decimate multitudes of humanity merely to seek temporal power and glory.

The irony of it all, is that while man is now breaking new ground in the pursuit of artificial intelligence, we are yet to unravel the secret to making peace. War and strife have forced millions of people to other shores worrying governments in the West about the security of their borders. The diversity of faiths can be a boon to a globalised world, yet bigots think of religious diversity as a threat to their sovereignty. We are yet to come to terms with the "clash of civilizations."

All of this comes at a time when a nationalist ideology is pushing back globalization and consolidating the doctrine of the preservation and advancement of national glory, one that is insouciant to another world outside one's borders. That's a scary déjà vu. None of us wants a 1939 world stage setting that brought disaster on the planet.

Already we see the primacy of democracy waning as a couple of countries in Europe and south Asia slip gradually into authoritarian governance, a consequence of a hard-core nationalist revival. So, this book seeks to prick the ear and invite global communities to seek the peaceful advancement of humanity that globalisation can bring about and open the gates to a common future, casting away the other troubles that nationalist ideologies trigger.

In that haven, globalism and literacy will ultimately rid the world of the migrant conundrum and the perceived troubles with religious diversity, bring about a new optimal literacy threshold, and open the world to a new morality, which will engender a climate in which the notion of war will be scorned and the peoples of the planet will embrace the one world, one humanity doctrine.

PART I

A Prelude

Another World Somewhere[1] is a fictional narrative and paints a not-quite-inconceivable future for a world that does not care to share it with everybody on the planet.

---

[1] *Unless otherwise indicated, all the names, characters, businesses, places, events and incidents in this book are either the product of the author's imagination or used in a fictitious manner. Any resemblance to actual persons, living or dead, or actual events is purely coincidental.*

Another World Somewhere

Amarjit is watching the cricket finals at England's Lord's, screening on television across the world. The game is about to end in a photo-finish. India has to score 143 runs with three wickets in hand, if it must take the coveted trophy. This is a nail-biting situation. Amarjit is stressed.

His buddy and dorm roommate, Bill, isn't a cricket fan. Yes, he is crazy about baseball, but Amarjit always riled him up saying: "Baseball is a poor man's cricket game." Of course, he wouldn't bother with that.

So, that evening, as Amarjit was switching on that tv channel, Bill ran his eyes across his mate's impressive library and stopped to open the pages of a new title on that shelf: "A New World Somewhere." It's a book about the planet Shroud, one of the several planets in our solar system.

The game is about to begin – the English captain is setting the field and Amarjit, intoxicated with cricket, is oblivious of Bill's presence in the room. He flops on a bed and stretches out his legs, tearing a bag of popcorn open. Bill chooses to open the book and browse on another couch.

Shroud was one of the many planets in our solar system. It's surface area of 144.4 million kilometres squared was a third the size of our own planet Earth. It was terrestrial, although cold. It had seasons, canyons and weather conditions. The planet was older than our own and its atmosphere was composed of the regular elements that made it very hospitable to life. Quite like the earth, its oceans once blanketed almost 70 percent of the planet's surface area, and streams of rivers and lakes flowed gently across its ecology.

Little is known about its early civilisation, other than the notion that early sapiens on Shroud were anatomically similar in their characteristics to humans who colonised the earth some 25,000 years ago. It is believed that during the earth's Upper Paleolithic period, some populations on planet Shroud moved from a wandering lifestyle of hunting and gathering to occupations like farming and gradually developed social organization and invented writing in the corresponding Neolithic era.

With the expanse of time, 20,000 years later, Shroud's people, by a process of evolution, had acquired civilized phenotypes or traits and had made some advancement in thought and organization as

Part I: A Prelude

well as in the sciences and medicine. Its population was gradually categorized as multifarious in culture, tradition and custom, language and religion. In many ways, Shroud's advancement was just a step ahead of the progress made by man on earth back in the day. Nation states evolved, organized on a tribal model, and were created to serve their peoples brought together by commonalities.

Those taking up residence in the colder regions in the Western hemisphere of Shroud were fair-skinned and colonised the continent Eureka. The light-skinned tribes chose habitats in the middle and Eastern regions on the continent Aplasia and the dark-skinned communities settled in warmer climes on arid land in the middle-south, on the continent Hakuna Matata. In time, Shroud provided habitat in five vast continents, and its peoples – vastly diverse - multiplied.

Amarjit, jumped out of his bed, yelling and throwing up his hands, and flaunting a thumbs-up with a closed fist. Bill was distracted. He put his book down.

"Buddy, what's going on?"

Amarjit opened the freezer and grabbed an ice-cream cone.

"Shirodkar has scooped a long shot over the boundary."

He then jumped into bed and stared at the screen, cheering flag-waving Indians at Lord's.

Bill had made a mental switch by then.

All of Shroud's people were congenitally similar, although their tribal customs and traditions on the continents were distinctly unique. Those on the continent Hakuna Matata were scantily clad in the rural regions, and their customs were out on their own. A prospective groom would make a payment to the father of his bride to compensate for the loss of his daughter. The compensation was not a payment made in cash but instead in the gifting of cattle. In many nation states, on Hakuna Matata, female genital mutilation was widely practiced. Their conflicts were militant, but mostly tribe-driven.

In Southeast Aplasia, some nation states practiced widow-burning. A woman made widow after the death of her husband would throw herself on to her husband's pyre and burn to death.

In prehistoric Eureka as well as in Amuruk - a powerful nation separated from Eureka by an ocean, early tribes initially made weapons out of stone. But after the age of mechanization, battles were fought with double barrel guns, thus giving Eurekan and Amurukan soldiers a head-start over their counterparts from other continents in the mid-Eastern parts of Shroud.

All these tribes embraced religions into which they were born, and those included tribes acknowledging the Creator of the universe as the Sovereign Lord, tribes idol worshipping, and tribes that were pagan – or atheist – who dismissed any talk of a Creator-God as man's delusion.

The five continents on Shroud were: Eureka, Aplasia, Hakuna Matata, Amuruk and Arabi. The earliest settlers on Amuruk leaned toward a cosmic identity in their primary belief – seeking interconnectedness between the individual and his environs, his tribe, the soil and ultimately with the Great Spirit. The timelessness of nature and its gifts to mankind had been at the core of Amurukan beliefs. This connectedness defined eternity. Absolute respect for the gift of nature was at the heart of this religious practice.

The progress of these communities in time led to the establishment of fledgling schools, a trading currency, and the development of agricultural tools for the production of grain. Then with the advance of years and of a growing literate society, man's creative instincts led to the development of mechanization, initially in the West of Shroud on the continents of Eureka and Amuruk.

This revolution in manufacturing of goods spread to other nations and provided jobs to millions of people. It was then time for a more efficient banking system to develop, and it did. In time, the revolution led to an advancement in transportation systems for the moving of goods as trains and aircraft production opened the doors to people connecting and trading worldwide.

With progress, came ambitions and greed, and with those traits, man's desire to grab power and territories advanced. The manufacturing of weapons had begun. In tandem, conflict among communities seeking habitat on lands populated by people of similar traditions began to break out.

Amarjit sprung up in excitement again, swinging his hands and banging the doors of his room. He nipped across to the fridge and grabbed a Coke.

"We're getting there, buddy. Just a matter of time," he prophesied.

Part I: A Prelude

Bill signalled a thumbs-up and buried his head into the book again.

In Eureka, the desire of the Slazic people to leave Astra- Hussar - a nation state in central Eureka - and be part of Zdravo, sparked a revolt. Zdravo, a neighbouring state, was home to people of custom and traditions akin to those of the Slazic people. In rapid succession, events took a violent turn. A freedom fighter from Zdravo pulled the trigger on Duke Felix, heir to the throne of Astra -Hussar, and that provoked a war.

The continent by then had stockpiles of arms and ammunition. It was just as well that countries within Eureka had made mutual defense agreements which guaranteed defence support to any country within the alliance or group of nations. In other words, if Astra-Hussar was attacked, other countries in the group would come to its defence. The alliance agreements were binding, and swiftly the Prime powers, including Astra-Hussar, Gutentag, and the Truckman Empire, went to war with Supreme powers including Brighton, la France, Roulette, Jugemu - a nation state on the eastern hemisphere - and Amaruk. That war was fought for over three years, and some forty million people either perished or were wounded.

Two decades later, there were three important developments, one of which was cataclysmic. First, William Watson, the President of Amaruk at the time, the wealthiest and most weaponised nation state on Shroud, drew up a plan to unite all nations on the planet and set up an assembly of diplomats representing every nation state to speak in the interest of his or her country. This assembly was named *Humanity*. At least 190 nations enrolled as member states of this global body.

At about the same time as people across the planet Shroud were picking up the pieces of a devastating war, a smart man, Thomas Kenneth, presented a theory for the creation of wealth. This was a capitalist theory which set out a model for how nation states could organise the manufacturing and services industry to generate employment and multiply wealth.

But peace on the planet was broken a second time. This third development was a gigantic shocker. An ambitious military man, Hans, who had risen to the top ranks of the military in Gutentag in Eureka, grabbed power, declared himself emperor, and invaded neighbouring Polska.

As a young lad, Hans refused to conform to school discipline and would often run into arguments with his father, who beat him severely. Hans dropped out of middle school. His father died early, and with his mother passing away when he was 18, the young man was driven to homeless shelters and did casual labour for a living. He later joined the county's military. The unfortunate circumstances of his youth had made him a hardened and brutal man.

After Gutentag was humiliated in the first global war on Shroud, Hans had moved up the ranks in the military, got into politics, and declared that his country's mission was two-fold: the first would be to wipe out a complete race representing Shroud's earliest faith group, who then populated this central-western part of this vast continent, and second, take control of the rest of Eureka, comprising several nations.

The invasion of Polska provoked Brighton and la France, who in a gesture to honor their defence agreement with an ally, declared war on Gutentag. As other state groupings joined the war in defence of alliance partners, conflict and strife, death and destruction gripped the planet. The war dragged on.

Jakub, a young Polskan who came from Shroud's earliest faith groups, was a lad of ten when Gutentag soldiers invaded his hometown – a village in the south of the country – dragged his family and several other families out of their homes and put them on trains bound for a killing field. Upon arrival at this destination of death, soldiers broke up families and dispersed them to different camps. Jakub was out on his own, after his family was snatched away from him and sent to the gallows, archeological reports revealed.

The boy was put to work in one of the labour camps, building crematoriums where hundreds of people were being burnt every day. He was whipped and tortured if he was ever seen taking a break from his work. Jakub fortunately survived several death marches.

The war, anyway, dragged on and Gutentag soldiers were growing war weary. It was just as well that allied nations finally carried out the largest seaborne invasion in Shroud's history. The operation began the liberation of la France and later Western Eureka. Hans was desperate. He was cornered, and his arrest was only a matter of time. He chose to bite the bullet and killed himself. Gutentag's generals then surrendered. Several generals were consumed by the war, and their lieutenants were arrested and hanged.

But Jugemu refused unconditional surrender to the Supreme forces. Henry Tremain, Amaruk's President at the time, weary of war and seeking an end to it, ordered the bombing of two Jugemu cities. This was the first nuclear bomb ever to be dropped on Shroud, and Jugemu was razed to the ground, archaeological reports affirm. The country's broken government then unconditionally surrendered to Amaruk's generals, and that put an end to Shroud's second war. At the end of this war, some 75 million people perished. Shroud was in a state of shock.

The drift into history was beginning to grip Bill's interest. He gently turned on his side to check on Amarjit. His buddy was solemn, focussed, and silent.

"He's best left to his own devices," Bill muttered. Then he buried his head in his book again.

Nation states, especially on Eureka, were paralyzed by the destruction of roads and bridges, telephone cables, railway tracks, the breaking down of transportation and communications systems, damage to industrial equipment and technology, the soaring unemployment of workers, and a shattered economy. But picking up the pieces, they rose from the ashes.

After the second war, Kenneth's model of a capitalist theory met with great success and nation states in the Western hemisphere acquired wealth, leaving other nations to themselves to create their own economic models. Consequently, some nations chose to be egalitarian societies, like communist societies on our planet, and adopted an economic model in which all people would be equal. A man would work as best as he could with his skills and talents and would receive from the state a payment only as much as to cover his basic needs of food, clothing, and shelter.

In the hot and arid regions of the continent Arabi, citizens of those nations adopted theocracy as the basis for the enactment of laws. Their laws were made in accordance with the teachings of their religion. These were regions where oil generated the greater part of their national wealth. Their exports were the result of oil-fuelled industrial development in the West, and that was a win-win, situation.

In many eastern states, where literacy was not optimal and growing very gradually, prosperity came to only those who were literate. The less literate population fell below the poverty line in most of these countries in the East and accounted for half or more of the total population on Shroud. Consequently, the planet Shroud was divided into blocs. The countries in the East and Southwest regions, where literacy levels were low, were grappling with the problems commonly seen in low-income countries precisely because national budgets, in greater proportion, were diverted to defence weapons, and only the crumbs of national budgets were disbursed to education and social welfare.

In these regions of Shroud, poverty was part of a vicious cycle that brought in its wake growing illiteracy, theft, violence, beggary, population explosion, squatters' colonies, sickness and disease, and so forth. In nations like these, where gaps between the rich and poor were widening, an atmosphere of despair was taking root. Literary citizens thus looked outside their state borders toward Western nations to establish habitats and offer their skills and training. This suited nations in the West, where ageing populations were preventing capitalist growth of national economies.

All this was fine when the migration benefit was two-sided and mutually beneficial. But as civilization seemingly progressed, after the second war on Shroud, less developed nations began to secretly expand their weaponry in preparedness to defend themselves, and a race for the building of nuclear weapons gradually developed. In the next couple of decades, poorer countries acquired nuclear technology, too, in secret, and the greater part of Shroud was then nuclear-armed to bring about death and destruction in the event of conflict with an enemy nation.

The greed for power and supremacy as well as for the conquest of rich neighbouring territory drove strong men and dictators of some nation states to engage in war rhetoric and ultimately in war. The Security Council at *Humanity* often stepped in with peace proposals, but most of them were an exercise in failure, and war brought about death, destruction and the flight of millions of refugees. That scale of combat was seen in several regions of Shroud, especially on the Arabi and Hakuna Matata continents: some driven by tribal troubles, others seeking oil-rich neighbouring territory, and yet others protesting to bring down their dictators.

The civil war in Safari, a country in the eastern region of Hakuna Matata was terrible and deadly.

Aisha's child was nine days old when a gang of looters broke into her house and seized her husband. "They wanted all our money and my jewellery," she told a news reporter, according to archival reports. "I said I would give anything for my husband's life. But they shot him in the head, buried him in the backyard, and left."

A couple of days later, Aisha's father's house was blown up, and as the bloody civil war penetrated the neighbouring villages, her family chose to flee. Her husband's people fled to Mahaba, and she began the long journey across the border to Hewale.

"The war was traumatic," Aisha told that reporter. "Every couple of steps along the way we saw blood and death."

At about the same time, in the Arabi regions of Shroud, several nation-states were engaged in war. Soran, a farmer from a village in Ishq, told a news reporter that he woke up terrorized one morning having learnt that some 5,000 people in the neighbouring villages of Ma'an were killed in a chemical poison attack ordered by the country's President Sultan to eliminate a particular ethnic population. That day Soran saw some 40,000 people, like an ocean of humanity, making a silent exodus out of Ishq and a forced entry into the neighbouring country Turgay.

"It was impossible to stay back. Sultan's army was shooting men and taking their wives and children away to be left at camps," he told a reporter after the war. "I ordered my mother, wife, and nine children to rise and leave."

Soran's exodus was like an unending saga of trials and tribulation. His daughter was lost in the melee one night, forcing him to make a sinuous retreat. On his way back, he lost his mother, but reunited again in Turgay. They continued the trek only through the night and hid in the caves of surrounding hills in the day to avoid being seen by Sultan's soldiers. His cousin's wife was about to deliver a baby but also had to deal with her 18-month child in arms about to die. The scourge of war in the Arabi and Hakuna Matata continents especially brought on an uninterrupted exodus of refugees fleeing to nations in the Western hemisphere. When their count crossed the 100 million mark, western nations shut their borders and erected red flags, forcing riots, chaos, and confusion.

Bill turned to check on Amarjit again and noticed the boy was now fast asleep – occasionally muttering some cricket jargon:

"Superstar Shirodkar!!! Did you have to get off that crease???

Bill chuckled and turned to his book again.

Not surprisingly, groups of ultra-nationalists: racists and white supremacists, politicians and bigots intolerant of eastern religions, emerged on the political stage in the West of Shroud, threatened by the fact that people of different faiths, skin colour, tradition, and custom would steal the supreme identity of Eureka. There were calls from allies of western nations to stop the boats on which refugees would take a ride to Western shores. These politicians ordered their border agents to seize cash and other assets from refugees to pay for their maintenance. The Prime Minister of Hussar ranted about the fact that these refugees practiced an alien religion and would alter the identity of his nation's culture.

It was about the time Amaruk was going to the polls. Tom Crunch won it by the skin of his teeth, and his people cheered, popping champagne bottles at parties across the country. Crunch promised to bring glory back to Amaruk: keep foreigners away from his country's borders, and regulate the entry of people of some faiths.

Away from Amuruk, a new nationalist ideology was emerging in Hussar and Polska on Eureka's continent as well as in a couple of countries in Aplasia. In tandem, the erstwhile democratic traditions eroded and waned in these regions on Shroud. A parting of ways between political leaders on these continents opened the way to the creation of alliances, and political rhetoric kept these countries in the throes of an impending gloom. An overwhelming fear of a nuclear war gripped nations on Shroud.

There were sobering voices as well, calling for globalisation of the planet, tolerance of the flight of refugees to Western shores, the respect for human rights, the embrace of interfaith discourse, and the recognition of the peace that discourse can engender. Globalisation theorists spoke of the cause of brotherhood, of creating one world, one humanity. At conferences and summits hosted by *Humanity*, which drew delegates from all over the world, speakers shared thoughts on "common responsibility" for a "common future." A common thread at these conferences warned delegates that we must live together as one, because if we don't, we will die together. But calls for a globalised world fell on deaf ears.

Part I: A Prelude

Archeological reports confirm that Shroud's 12 sovereign nations had publicly announced successful detonation of nuclear weapons. It also affirmed that the total inventory of warheads on Shroud had reached an all-time high and that a significant proportion of that stockpile was deployed with missiles and aircraft and kept in a state of high operational alert. There were reports, too, of poorer nations developing nuclear weapons and of new military alliances forming. *Armageddon* was on the lips of millions of people on Shroud. That was apparently the calm before the storm.

In quick succession then, the planet was troubled with conflicts erupting on most of its hemispheres. Tensions heightened as a state in West Aplasia took as hostages some fifteen Eurekan citizens as leverage for political bargaining. In Hakuna Matata, yet another coup was staged, this time by the military chief of Mojo on the western flank who took the reins of power after deposing Mojo's President. In the Southeast of Eureka, an exodus of thousands of ethnic peoples were fleeing Gözel. Most countries in Aplasia and Eureka declared a state of emergency.

Finally, that night some despot on Shroud hit the nuclear button, and warheads were roaring across the planet. That prompted new military allies to unite and destroy their enemies. There was chaos everywhere—missiles were shot at strategic positions in key countries across the five continents as the conflict spread like wildfire and allies were roped into this deadly war.

Humanity's Chief urged calm. The shares on stock markets across the planet dived down. The prices of food and commodities hit the roof. Corporate giants shut down, and as thousands of millions of ordinary people perished, staunch patriots were fighting with sticks and stones. Nations were burning everywhere as a nuclear holocaust unfolded. Almost all of Shroud's land surface had become inhabitable by nuclear radiation, causing in time the collapse of civilization and the extinction of humanity and of all biological life on the planet.

In the end, Shroud was silenced. Then, almost five thousand years later, after that bloody war on the planet, an Earth scientist, G. Vincenzo, discovered Shroud on his telescope in 1610 and gave it a new name: MARS.

Bill put his book down.

"That's some twist to the tale," he thought.

The silence in the room was eerie. The only sound around him came from the ticking of the clock. So, he rose from the bed. He turned to Amarjit who was now in deep slumber. He put the book back on the shelf and tip-toed out of the room.

"Hmmmm." He pondered.

PART II

Think Globally

UBUNTU

'UBUNTU' in the Xhosa culture means:
"I am because we are".

Chapter 1

The Troubles with Nationalism
A Distasteful Déjà Vu

These are scary times, almost reminiscent of that holocaust of the first half of the last century which eliminated some 110 million people in two world wars. If this seems like an exaggeration, consider Cass R. Sunstein's *It Can Happen Here* and the reports he presents of the eerie silence that lingered across Hitler's Germany as his evil designs were about to be unleashed to thrust the world into a state of shock, traumatized by blood and destruction evidenced across the planet.

A draconian world stage in the late thirties was all set for the explosion of evil: The Axis alliance with tyrants in Italy, Japan, and Germany pitched on one side against principal Allied powers Great Britain, the United States, and the Soviet Union. Italy invaded Ethiopia in October 1935. Japan had already taken Manchuria, and by 1937 controlled large swathes of China. Germany ramped up its prewar expansion in 1938 with the annexation of Austria. The rest of it is dreaded history.

The stakes today may be different, but the troubles are the same. The greed for power, the abhorrence of a foreign workforce, the intolerance of alien faiths within one's borders, and the desire for national glory are driving Europe and the United States to tighten security at their borders. That's some writing on the wall. What are the signs?

The greater part of the world is presumably aware that today eight sovereign states on our planet have publicly announced successful detonation of nuclear weapons, those being the United States, Russia, the UK, France, China, India, Pakistan, and North Korea.[1]

The Stockholm International Peace Research Institute (SIPRI) affirms that the worldwide total inventory of nuclear weapons as of 2021 stood at 13,080.[2] Russia and the USA together possess over 90 per cent of all those weapons.[3] In a Press Release issued on 12 June 23 to coincide with the release of the SIPRI Yearbook, it said that of the total global inventory of an estimated 12,512 warheads in January 2023, about 9,576 were in military stockpiles for potential use. Of those, an estimated 3,844 warheads were deployed with missiles and aircraft, and around 2,000—nearly all of which belonged to Russia or the USA—were kept in a state of high operational alert, meaning that they were fitted to missiles or held at airbases hosting nuclear bombers.[4]

Furthermore, according to an earlier Press Release issued by SIPRI on 24 April, 2023, the world's total military expenditure increased by 3.7 per cent in real terms in 2022, to reach a new high of $2,240 billion. Military expenditure in Europe saw its steepest year-on-year increase in at least 30 years. The three largest spenders in 2022—the United States, China, and Russia—accounted for 56 per cent of the world total, according to new data on global military spending published by SIPRI.[5]

Now, alongside, we see other developments as well – the most important being the fact that new alliances are forming and consolidating. That is some writing on the wall. The other worrying factor is this fast-unfolding, self-preservationist doctrine which seeks to obsessively engage countries in keeping their neighbours or people of other faiths and cultures outside their fences. Fair enough. It is worrying to see people gate-crashing through your borders without legal documents. But the policing of the borders at migrant recipient countries has been sometimes rough. The people fleeing Honduras, Guatemala, and El Salvador, after all, are those fleeing violence, persecution, and poverty in their home countries. So are hapless refugees from other war-torn countries.

In a speech in September 2023 at a conference of bishops in the French port city of Marseille, Pope Francis proclaimed: "Those who risk their lives at sea, do not invade, they look for welcome."

In the ongoing pages of this book, I carry the insightful thoughts of Francois Crepeau, the UN Special Rapporteur on the Human Rights of Migrants, which he shared at a European Union Summit a few years ago. He had proposed that the European Union must recognize that irregular migration is a result of policies that prohibit immigration. That is because the forbidden fruit is what drives us all to repel and counter-challenge. But let's examine his proposals later in our chapter on globalization.

A sweeping view of the political landscape that emerged in Europe and in the United States of America some years ago made it almost worrying to think of how fast and furiously the ideas of bigots and demagogues were beginning to influence voter electorates in the West to create isolated havens settled by people of "pure Aryan races." The two World Wars of the last century were fought precisely for that ideological haven.

An extremist nationalist ethos now seems to me the most damning for any hope of a globalized planet that seeks peace.

While the Brexit catapult and the racial rumblings in Europe were already painting a dim future for the world in the middle of the last decade, former American President Donald Trump, speaking at the 73rd session of the UN General Assembly in September, 2018, dumped the global cooperation idea. "We reject the ideology of globalism, and we embrace the doctrine of patriotism," he said. "Around the world, responsible nations must defend against threats to sovereignty not just from global governance, but also from other, new forms of coercion and domination."[6]

It's just as well that on November 11, 2018, French President Emmanuel Macron sounded a note of sobriety and told world leaders who converged on Paris for the centenary of the World War One Armistice, they must reject nationalism outright, describing it as a 'betrayal of patriotism.' Macron went on to say: "By saying 'our interests first and never mind the others,' you stamp out the most precious thing a nation has –

its moral values."⁷ Former German Chancellor Angela Merkel nodded in agreement and echoed the same political sentiment. Thank heavens for angels in our troubled world.

In a referendum on 23 June 2016, Brexit took the world by surprise. Almost 52 percent of the participating UK electorate voted to leave the EU, overthrowing Britain's relationship with its European neighbors in what was unequivocally some political upheaval.⁸ That was probably the first open demonstration of irritation festering within right wing western electorates at the rapidly growing migration of people to their shores.

Anger over Europe's liberal immigration policy may have been brewing for a long time. But in early 2012 that festering anger among European right wingers simply exploded, and we stood by as lone wolf terrorist attacks on the continent shocked us all – the bestial shooting on the island of Utøya in Norway by Anders Behring Breivik was just one of them.⁹

In the Netherlands, ahead of parliamentary elections in 2017, a leader in the House of Representatives had presented a set of proposals which included banning migrants from Islamic countries and closing mosques, Islamic schools, and asylum centres.¹⁰

In June 2018, Austria said it would close seven mosques and expel imams who, it said, are funded by foreign countries.[11] Now the immigration rules in Denmark are probably among Europe's toughest. The country reportedly allows its police to seize the property of migrants to pay for their upkeep and wants to boost contraception aid to developing countries to "limit the migration pressure."[12]

Making a point about this emergence of a new right-wing nationalist culture, the Human Rights Chief Zeid Ra'ad Al Hussein observed: "What Mr. Wilders shares in common with Trump, Mr. Orban, Mr. Zeman, Mr. Hofer, Mr. Fico, Madame Le Pen, Mr. Farage, he also shares with Da'esh (ISIS). All seek in varying degrees to recover a past, a halcyon so pure in form, where sunlit fields are settled by peoples united by ethnicity or religion, living peacefully in isolation, pilots of their fate, free of crime, foreign influence and war."[13]

A rising tide of this ultra-nationalist ethos actually stares us in the face and is witnessed in so many parts of the world where charismatic politicians dig their heels deep in the corridors of power. Consequently, as pressure from democratic blocks wane, there is now widespread talk of a democratic erosion in parts of Europe, namely Turkey, Poland and Hungary, and on the Asian continent, including the Philippines.

In a quiet moment, it's nice to think about how and why this came to pass and what's the way out of this rabbit hole?

The history of conflict on the planet is a narrative of how the marginalized, the plebeian, rank and file masses have turned against the bourgeoisie – our capitalist societies. So, it's reasonable to say that the rich and poor world can never ever co-exist without ineluctable conflict because extravagant and wasteful societies incite an irascible response from the poorer world. There must be committed engagement by rich nations with societies down south of the globe because a common future for all can come only with the common responsibility of all.

Consider expanding the notional scope of what globalisation can do to create a better, safer, and more just world and be cognizant of the fact that should the richer half of the planet choose instead to ignore and neglect this other half, global poverty will come back to haunt us. There are no "quick fixes" to sorting out the mess we are trapped in. Walls will not keep festering anger lying servile within. That anger will likely explode and break down walls.

In 2016, we saw an ocean of displaced humanity flock to European shores from war-torn Syria. In 2022, we saw caravans of about 5,000 South Americans fleeing poverty, violence, and persecution in the Honduras, Guatemala and El Salvador. A civilized nation cannot turn to actions that dehumanize the marginalized, seeking refuge at their borders.

A careful examination of what lies at the root of all this trouble might reveal the fact that migration is merely driven by poverty, the absence of opportunity, and the curse of terrorist violence and war primed by sectarian strife and nationalist ambitions that push the plebeian, the marginalized, and the rank and file to pile up on boats and take those dangerous journeys to western shores.

Martin Luther King, Jr., said it in fewer words: "We must learn to live together as brothers or perish together as fools."

Is globalisation key to redeeming the crisis? Let's see.

Chapter 2

Globalisation is not optional.
We either live together or die together.

The allegory of the long spoons, which makes a subtle point about "common responsibility" and a "common future," is a parable attributed to Rabbi Romshishok. Think of diners sitting on two sides of a long table on which delectable food waits. The guests at the table have extremely long spoons making it impossible for them to scoop up the food and drop it into their mouths. So, what does one do? The parable suggests that people on one side of that table have the opportunity to reach food out to the others on the other side of the table, so that in feeding one another, all are fed and no one is hungry.

Globalization, as an idea for cooperation among nations, may have emerged as a direct result of the Industrial Revolution, but in the post World War II era it got its shot-in-the arm with the giant leap in communications that rapid developments in information technology sprung on the world. This increase in global interaction, as everyone knows, prompted a growth in international trade and the exchange of ideas, beliefs, and culture.

Now, I am not going to sing to the choir but must warn that no man is an island. An extremely inward-looking political outlook that pursues the quest for isolation and the preservation of an illusory idea of supremacy is out of place in a world that seeks a common future.

Global post-war economic resurgence was essentially an outcome of brave thinking by the world community of economists and intellectuals who laid down the framework for international monetary policy, commerce, and finance and the founding of several international institutions intended to facilitate economic growth by lowering trade barriers. The General Agreement on Tariffs and Trade (GATT) tossed aside trade restrictions, giving way to the formation of the World Trade Organization (WTO). As a result, exports doubled from 8.5 percent of total gross world product in 1970 to 16.2 percent in 2001.[1]

It opens the gates to peace

East-West relations have in the last couple of decades been tepid, driven by what some observers attribute to Western hegemony, the failure to successfully mediate Palestinian - Israeli peace, the mutual distrust of religious affiliations, and the "clash of civilizations," which is the elephant in the room.

A globalized culture that opens the way to trade can break these barriers of mistrust by active technology transfers and the sharing of resources. In doing so, it can open the gates to peace. International trade is a great leveller, and there is evidence of what trade groupings have achieved hitherto.

Canada now has an ambitious target of ramping up the newcomer arrival count to 1.5 million over three years. In 2022, it welcomed 431,645 newcomers – an all-time high.[2] Now even in smaller provinces such as Nova Scotia, one can see the face of the region dramatically changed. There is evidence of social inclusion, and one can already see societal integration. People movement is a boon in a globalized world. It opens new opportunities in cultural understanding, which impact intercultural trade and business. As the domino effect intensifies between peoples of different cultures, interstate trading partners develop, distrust cautiously simmers and fades away. All this opens the gates to peace at a state level.

If we truly believe we are one world, one humanity, one people with a common destiny and a shared responsibility, we must hasten to open our windows on the world and embrace the opportunity of giving peace a chance through active globalisation.

Chapter 3

Migration is a Catalyst

The migration of people is an opportunity that must be seized if one is to witness the flourishing of a globalised society. That is because the movement of people comes with a reservoir of resource skills, which replaces an ageing workforce, raises the tax base, increases consumption, and creates wealth in the economy.

But, somehow, small but influential, nationalist segments of the population in Europe and the United States do not recognize that as an opportunity and have traditionally greeted newcomers with caution and suspicion. That notwithstanding, in the period between 1965 and 1990, the proportion of the labor force migrating approximately doubled. Most migration occurred among the developed countries and Less Developed Countries (LDCs).[1] The movement of doctors and medical personnel, software engineers and technical specialists in several sectors pushed the economies of Australia, Europe, Canada, and the United States to new highs. This came about at a time when these continents were looking to supplement an ageing population and were clamouring for new skills to stay competitive in a fast-changing technological economy.

As economic integration intensified, workers moved to areas with higher wages and most of the developing world leaned toward the international market. In 2016, partners in NAFTA (North American Free Trade Agreement) represented 28 percent of the world's gross domestic product (GDP) with just less than seven percent of the world's population.[2] The collapse of the Soviet Union ended the Cold War's division of the world, opening a gigantic free market.

In the last several decades, nation states have come together to cooperate in trade and economic activity to create more powerful representations in the global community. The European Union (EU) is the world's largest trading bloc and the second largest economy in the world. It is also the European Free Trade Association's largest trading partner. NAFTA, which binds the US, Canada, and Mexico to special trade agreements, is the world's largest free trade area. The 21-member economies of APEC (Asia Pacific Economic Cooperation) are home to around 2.9 billion people, and in 2018 represented approximately 60 percent of world GDP and 48 percent of world trade.[3]

Despairingly, the economies in the less developed countries have all along relied on loans and aid from Western monetary institutions, including the IMF and the World Bank, who have granted loans to these nations after imposing structural adjustment programs - with a vested interest - on them. But going by reports critical of the loan programs, these financial institutions had merely made veteran borrowers of the developing countries with the costs of debt servicing exceeding their capacity to repay and thus threatening a global financial crisis. Nothing great had changed Africa, anyway. The loan programs were, as critics claim, not an endeavour to globalise economies and raise the wealth of developing nations. They inherently failed because of a conflict of interest. The donor world was doling out financial aid without technological partnerships. That turned the loan program into an exercise in failure.

What the World Trade Organization has shown is that precisely by breaking down barriers or by trade groupings as in NAFTA national economies are able to forge ahead with greater pace. The idea of a world commonwealth is not new. It was the inspiration behind the founding of the League of Nations. The creation of the European Union was a great idea. Similar economic blocs can bring about that change we seek.

But if migration must be the catalyst in the globalization process, immigrant recipient countries will have to be welcoming. That welcome must be seen and felt in the design of one's cities, in the policing of multicultural societies, in social and political inclusion, and in religious tolerance.

Professor Sohail Inayatullah, a political scientist, observes: "Historically, the image of the city has gone from the city beautiful, focused on parklands and clean streets to the city ecological." Geneva, he says, has taken a different tack. "What was once a classical, traditionally white Euro city, has in the last forty years, transformed beyond belief." I have had the opportunity to see that new smart city. It now has a credible multicultural face with cafes lined with African, Middle-Eastern, Italian, Indian, and fast food restaurants, and in public life one sees a slew of cultures mixing.

But what is a multicultural city? Inayatullah tells us: "First it means city spaces are not segregated by race or gender, one should not be able to identify an ethnic area, or at least not see it in a negative way. Second, citizens should feel they are part of the city, that they are not discriminated against, especially by those in authority. But a multicultural city is also about incorporating other ways of knowing, of creating a complex and chaotic model of space, such that the city does not necessarily match the values of only one culture - example, mosques with temples and banks."[4]

The need for vibrant social inclusion that will generate social capital and preclude the mushrooming of ghettos of people of like cultures has fuelled debate across Canada. The importance of religion as an aspect of diversity has been increasing, too, since ultimately, ideological differences may prove more intractable than the racial divide which presently concerns policymakers.

It's important to realize that immigration is about people and therefore of the heart. "How we respond to the challenges of immigration, diversity and population change will literally determine whether we as a society live or die." That was a somewhat shocking statement made sometime ago by Brian Lee Crowley, the founding President of the Atlantic Institute for Market Studies (AIMS) in Canada, back in the day.

As any immigrant knows, uprooting and moving on to lands of different cultures is not music to the ears. It can be traumatic. A great majority of newcomers talk of loneliness in the initial years of settlement and later of the lack of a sense of belonging. Crowley addressed that observation in an OpEd he wrote for my newspaper *Touch BASE* some years ago.

"Immigration is not chiefly a matter of jurisdiction, but of people and therefore of the heart," he wrote. "Immigrants are people who uproot themselves from their homes in search of a better life. Thus, immigrants tend to congregate in specific cities. People don't move to places they've never heard of, so one of the most powerful attractions for immigrants is whether there are people like them in a new community — people who have prospered there.

"Being made to feel wanted and welcome is thus the strongest pro-immigration policy there is. So, in order for immigration to move outside the big cities, we need to foster immigrant communities and not just welcome individual newcomers."

Political demographers warn against emerging ghettos that may precipitate a culture of poverty where residents see no means of improving livelihood and become passive recipients of the welfare state. They speculate that these ghettos trap residents and their children into long term poverty and might even lead to social conflict.

"But social inclusion is also straightforward economics," says Howard Duncan, Chair Emeritus, International Metropolis Project. "Excluding newcomers from a place in their new society will reduce their ability to contribute to the labour market, to provide the innovation that diversity often is said to promise, and to put their entrepreneurial spirit to practice. Investing in immigration is only a first step. The real work comes with integration, and this must be practiced daily if a country is to succeed both economically and socially."[5]

A point to note is that social exclusion is sure to hinder the creation of social capital which is the basis of a society's prosperity. So, if we know what's good for us, we must choose to come together as a society and design multicultural city spaces that do not segregate by race or gender, nor identify an ethnic area.

The policing model, too, is being reconstructed in many other parts of the world to cope with the challenges of a multicultural society. The police jurisdictions in most countries in the West are believed to have long since shifted from an enforcement model to a community-responsive services model with an emerging focus on race relationships amid allegations of police discrimination.

In Canada, the recruitment pool in the police force now includes the best and brightest from our universities and from non-traditional groups in the country: Aboriginal, Asian, South Asian, and others. There are already open communication lines between the police and the Jewish and Islamic communities and through seminars with them, the police are now familiar with their customs and worship practice.

Chapter 4

Religious Diversity is a Boon, not a Threat

There is already evidence of an exponential growth in religious groups from South and East Asia, Africa, and the Middle East making their way to Europe, North America, and Australia. But the hundreds of thousands of newcomers who are headed to these countries every year are not going to leave their religion at the door and come in. That is because culture at its heart is religious.

The importing of skills from South and East Asia, Africa, and the Middle East is a pressing economic objective for governments in the West and the far South; therefore, the flow of newcomers to these countries is not an exercise in altruism. The United States, European nations, Australia, and New Zealand also recognise the desirability of a growing population to ramp up consumption, lift the tax base, and stay competitive. So, immigration is a big ticket item in the development plans of these rich nations, who recognise the importance of grabbing the opportunity and managing the challenge of religious pluralism at the same time.

Canada has had to examine the challenges and the opportunities of an immigration program with a comb's fine tooth. How does a country accommodate religious diversity and welcome an intellectual workforce of diverse cultures in a secular framework of governance? How do we grow multicultural cities? What are the perils of societal exclusion? How do we police in a multicultural society? What's the nature of identity politics? How do we deal with racial prejudice?

In the twenty-first century, Canada has especially been challenged by religious diversity with calls from Hindu disciples for a waterway to immerse the ashes of the deceased and calls, as well, from Muslims to include the Sharia law in Canada's penal code. Canada has confronted these challenges excellently.

There is, anyway, a significant demographic change in the world, characterized by considerable growth in the percentage of Westerners who are not Christian as well as an increase in Westerners reporting no religion, which is also a challenge. It cannot be denied that racial prejudice and religious intolerance are sticking points in this quagmire, and the problem is as old as the hills. Europe's experience with the movement of people has not been as rosy as it has been for Canada. But it may be fair to say that some European states have not been as welcoming.

In the last decade, Europe has had its share of hate crime and alongside a small but influential section of its society has lobbied to introduce legal barriers to stop admission of refugees to their countries. This, of course, was offset by former German Chancellor Angela Merkel's wisdom, who when challenged with an exodus of Syrian refugees, opened the country's borders wide to admit 1.1 million asylum seekers in 2015.[1]

In their desperation, Hungarian forces resorted to tear gas to disperse the crowds at their borders. There were rumblings of dissent at the time. Hungary's populist politicians had claimed for months that Europe was being overrun by refugees of different faiths who threaten to overwhelm their economy and security and alter its very culture and identity. Hungary was, indeed, being urged to halt its campaign portraying refugees as 'invaders'.[2]

The pace by then was set to roll back globalization. That was evident in the BREXIT call to "take back control" and the rallying call in the US to "make

America great again." The emergence of populists and demagogues especially in Britain and the United States impacted on global society, and that was unfortunate.

In the 2016 US election campaign, there was talk of barring the entry of citizens from seven Muslim-majority countries and of plans to build a wall to stop Mexicans from illegally crossing the US border, to put America first.[3]

So, to engage Canadians in this conversation, in 2011, I invited Father Raymond de Souza, a Roman Catholic priest of the Archdiocese of Kingston, Ontario, to deliver the keynote address at the first Spiritual Diversity Conference I convened in Halifax. Speaking on the topic, *The Challenge of Religious Diversity*, Father de Souza told delegates there were five dimensions to that perspective.

"First, religion has been a growing factor in global public life in the late 20th and early 21st century. This has an impact on Canadian public life as well, partly through immigration and partly through more assertive religious identity. Second, religious liberty is the first liberty and an essential public one, so any liberal democratic society has to make room for the religious in public life. Third, Canadian multiculturalism must take into account religious identity and practice, for culture at its heart is religious.

"Fourth, the diversity question is not about whether there is enough room for different religions, but whether there is room for religion at all. The battle as it were, is not between religions but between the aggressively secular and the religious. Lastly, the danger is this: the growth of secular fundamentalism in public life can be successful in marginalizing religious voices, but at the risk of radicalizing."

That is a lot to ponder.

Canada, anyway, has been pragmatic in the way it has approached these conundrums and is doing fairly well with a pluralist society. The Canadian government's news statement sometime ago confirmed that today one in three Canadian businesses is owned by an immigrant and one in four health care workers is a newcomer. Immigration accounts for almost 100 percent of Canada's labour force growth. Roughly three fourths of Canada's population growth comes from immigration, mostly in the economic category and according to government expectations, in 2036, immigrants will represent up to 30 percent of

Canada's population, compared with 20.7 percent in 2011.[4]

Indeed, immigration has changed the face of Canada. Today, immigrants make up 37 percent of pharmacists, 36 percent of physicians, 39 percent of dentists, 23 percent of registered nurses, and 35 percent of nurse aides and related occupations.[5]

So, while Canada's intake of refugees is altruistic, the country's immigration program is really driven by economic ambitions. The erstwhile whine about immigrants taking away jobs from Canadians and being a burden on the welfare system has faded away. The image of a lawyer, engineer, or doctor driving a taxi is surreal. Indeed, this was the challenge of change, and Canadians have met it head on. The newcomer today is an active participant in our democratic institutions.

Interfaith dialogue eases the way to a globalized world.

The ongoing dialogue of faith groups promoted through national and international conferences in the West has shown that people of diverse faiths can come together and become the critical solution to today's grave problems. Globalization has spurred the movement of people across borders for the greater good, and while migration of skills is a great opportunity to boost and diversify economies, there are, as discussed previously, some challenges that come in tow. A dialogue with faith groups, has shown that a lot of faith ignorance and prejudice can be dispelled by bringing people and faiths together. It's important to recognize that as people of different faiths take up residence in the West – and that will happen because immigration spurs economic growth – the challenge of accommodating religious diversity, especially within the framework of secular governance, gets more daunting.

So, between 2011 and 2016, I convened three Spiritual Diversity Conferences in Halifax, Canada, which brought delegates and religious scholars to the city from across North America to address the challenges that divide us as a people. These conferences were designed to seek commonalities as well as acknowledge differences and make a commitment to engage in civil discourse. The hope was to promote greater interfaith understanding with people affirming a respect for the religious beliefs of others, promoting egalitarianism and affirming respect, at the same time, for the country's core democratic values.

The conferences drew speakers from across North America, and we saw professors, theologians of all faiths, scientists and atheists converge on the city of Halifax to share thoughts on some of these grave matters.

Dr. Amir Hussain, a Professor at the Department of Theological Studies, Loyola Marymount University in Los Angeles, spoke to delegates at the 2013 Interfaith conference I had convened in the city and focused his remarks on religious divisions and social conflicts and used the metaphor of a "faith neighbour" to discuss his ideas. He opened his presentation with thoughts from Professor Wilfred Cantwell Smith, a former mentor and one of the greatest scholars of religion in the twentieth century.

One of Wilfred's most important books, he said, was the 1981 edition of *Towards a World Theology – Faith and the Comparative History of Religion,* in which he argued that our various religious traditions were best understood when taken together. "What they have in common is that the history of each has been what it has been in significant part because the history of the others has been what it has been."

To show the deep connections in our religious history, Professor Smith began the book with the story of Leo Tolstoy, his *Confession* written in 1879. Tolstoy's conversion was the story of Barlaam (the hermit) and Josaphat (the Indian prince). In the story, the Indian prince Josaphat is converted from a life of worldly power to the search for moral and spiritual truths by Barlaam, a Sinai desert monk.

Hussain told conference delegates: "Tolstoy learned the story from the Russian Orthodox Church. However, it was not a Russian story, as the Russian Church got it from the Byzantine Church. But it was not a Byzantine story, either, as it came to the Byzantine Church from the Muslims. But the story did not originate with Muslims, as Muslims in Central Asia learned it from Manichees, who got it from Buddhists,"

"The tale of Barlaam and Josaphat is, in fact, a story of the Buddha," he said. "Bodhisattva becomes 'Bodasaf' in Manichee, 'Josaphat' in later narratives of the tale. "However, Wilfred's genius was not in simply pointing to the history of this story, but to how it moved forward in time." Hussain went on to say that those who know Tolstoy know that he was an influence on a young Indian lawyer, Mahatma

Gandhi, who founded Tolstoy farm in Durban in 1910. "And those that know Gandhi know that the story does not end with him. Gandhi was an influence on a young African American minister, the Reverend Martin Luther King, Jr. The story shows that we are connected to each other, both forwards and backwards in time." He makes the point, excellently, that we are neighbours to each other.

Hussain tells of another narrative. "Someone once asked Wilfred: 'Professor Smith, are you Christian?' If the question had been: 'Are you *a* Christian' the answer would have been a very simple 'yes.'" He says Wilfred paused and thought about his answer. 'Am I Christian?' he said. 'Maybe, I was last week. On a Tuesday. At lunch. For about an hour. But if you really want to know, ask my neighbour.'"

He goes on to say that there are any number of conflicts with religious undertones that one can talk about – from Israel/Palestine, to the Balkans, to civil wars in Sri Lanka and the Congo. "But it's important to note that pluralism and dialogue are happening around the Muslim world, not just in North America. In 2007, based out of Jordan, several Muslim scholars, clerics, and intellectuals issued a call to

Christian leaders with the publication of the document "*A Common Word Between Us and You.*"

The document calls Christians and Muslims into dialogue based on the two great commandments in each tradition (Mark12:28-32): love of God and love of one's neighbour. "It is instructive for us to remember that when Jesus is asked about the greatest commandment, he repeats the words of the *Shema,* Deuteronomy 6:4 '*Hear O Israel, the Lord our God, the Lord is one.*'"

In his book *Our Last Best Chance: The pursuit of peace in a time of peril,* King Abdullah II of Jordan narrates how the document *A Common Word Between Us and You* became the most successful Muslim-Christian, interfaith initiative at the time. It, in fact, resulted in the convening of the first meeting of the Catholic-Muslim Forum held at the Vatican under the auspices of Pope Benedict XVI in 2008. The document was also instrumental in diffusing tensions globally after the pope's academic lecture in 2006 delivered at the University of Regensberg in Germany - in which he cited some negative comments of a fourteenth-century Byzantine emperor on Islam - sparked a major global controversy.

It may be said that interfaith dialogue is at the heart of the Christian message. Hussain refers to the parable of the Great Banquet in Matthew 25:31-46.

"When the son of man comes in His glory and all the holy angels with Him, then He will sit on the throne of His glory. All the nations will be gathered before Him and He will separate them one from another, as a shepherd divides his sheep from the goats. And He will set the sheep on His right hand, but the goats on the left. Then the King will say to those at his right hand, 'Come, you blessed of my Father, inherit the kingdom prepared for you from the foundation of the world: for I was hungry and you gave Me food; I was thirsty and you gave Me drink; I was a stranger and you took Me in; I was naked and you clothed Me; I was sick and you visited Me; I was in prison and you came to Me.'

"Then the righteous will answer Him saying, 'Lord, when did we see You hungry and feed You, and thirsty and give You drink? When did we see You a stranger and take You in, or naked and clothe You. Or when did we see You sick, or in prison and come to You?' And the king will answer and say to them: 'Assuredly, I say to you, inasmuch as you did it to one of the least of these My brethren, you did it to Me.'"

Hussain was making the point that in order to gain a seat at the banquet, we must do likewise: care for the stranger and be nice to our Muslim neighbours. "We can do this at the international or national level within our churches and mosques," he said. "Since 1980, the National Christian Muslim Liaison Committee has existed as an official vehicle of dialogue. Led by the United Church of Canada, there have been several conferences and workshops on interfaith dialogue. In 2004, the United Church published a study document entitled *That we may Know Each Other: United Church – Muslim Relations Today.*"

What can we do at the institutional level? Hussain says we can partner with individual mosques or Islamic centres. "There is the example of the Muslim Christian Consultative Group in Los Angeles. They have a new program *Standing Together,* which pairs churches and mosques. Through that work we can help each other to a better understanding of our traditions."

As religious people, we share a common belief that it is our duty to help one another, Hussain points out. "Someone asked a Christian minister about the quote from the *Book of Genesis*, in which God asks Cain about his brother Abel. Cain responds with the famous line: Am I my brother's keeper? This was to say: Am I responsible for him? However, this particular minister answered the question differently. "Am I my brother's keeper? Yes, I am, because I am my brother's brother."

The teachings of the Baha'i faith echo the same doctrine and call for the creation of one world, one humanity. In 1995, addressing the United Nations' World Summit for Social Development in Copenhagen, the Bahá'í community related this key principle to social development, stating: "The bedrock of a strategy that can engage the world's population in assuming responsibility for its collective destiny must be the consciousness of the oneness of human kind."

Bahá'u'lláh, the founder of the Bahá'í faith, wrote: "Regard man as a mine rich in gems of inestimable value. Education can, alone, cause it to reveal its treasures and enable mankind to benefit therefrom."

The Bahá'í scriptures proclaim: "Religion is the source of illumination, the cause of development and the animating impulse of all human advancement and has been the basis of all civilization and progress in the history of mankind. It is the source of meaning and hope for the vast majority of the planet's inhabitants and has a limitless power to inspire sacrifice, change and long-term commitment in its followers. It is, therefore, inconceivable that a peaceful and prosperous global society—a society which nourishes a spectacular diversity of cultures and nations—can be established and sustained without directly and substantively involving the world's great religions in its design and support."

Reverend Fr. Owen Connolly, assistant pastor at the Archdiocese of Halifax, speaking at the 2016 Interfaith conference hosted in the same city, focused on Jesus Christ's *Sermon on the Mount* to make the point that Christianity is not a label that one wears, but a life that one lives. He told delegates: "I was really struck some many years ago reading Mahatma Gandhi's philosophy of non-violence and learning that he based his teachings on the *Sermon on the Mount*. Gandhi was, of course, a devout Hindu and a great admirer of Jesus. He knew the teachings of Jesus better than most Christians of his era. This was also the inspiration for people like Desmond Tutu and Martin Luther King."

He then read out the words of the *Sermon on the Mount* from Matthew's gospel:

Blessed are the poor in spirit, for theirs is the kingdom of heaven. Blessed are they who mourn, for they will be comforted. Blessed are the meek, for they will inherit the land. Blessed are they who hunger and thirst for righteousness, for they will be satisfied. Blessed are the merciful, for they will be shown mercy. Blessed are the clean of heart, for they will see God. Blessed are the peacemakers, for they will be called children of God. Blessed are they who are persecuted for the sake of righteousness, for theirs is the kingdom of heaven.

Summing up his presentation, Connolly told delegates: "There are far too many Christians in the world today who want to come to the resurrection without going through the passion and death. Christianity is not a label that we wear but a life that we live."

But sustaining interfaith dialogue over time necessitates multifaith literacy that would enable us to move from tolerance to an ethic of coping with difference and complexity.

Syed Adnan Hussain, Assistant Professor of Religion at Saint Mary's University, speaking at the same conference told delegates that multifaith literacy is more than merely learning the facts about other faith traditions. "It is also attempting to engage with those traditions on their own terms. This logically requires that multifaith literacy begins with a suspension of the primacy of one's own truth claims."

A dialogue with faith groups at the national and international level should endeavour to arrive at two outcomes. First, we seek to deepen public understanding of different religious traditions, find commonalities, acknowledge differences, and advance an appreciation of the world's religious diversity. To these ends, a desired result would be greater societal harmony. Second, in examining challenges that pluralist societies face and understanding how interfaith dialogue can inform both social and security policy development, the desired results would be the drafting of policies that accommodate religious diversity.

·

Chapter 5

Literacy is Key to its Success

There are no quick fixes to the torment of our times. The development of literate societies, an overhauling of the nature of our ethos, the sharing of technology and resources with weaker nation states through a sterling globalized culture, and the creation of egalitarian societies may be the only way forward. The stakes are high. The global community needs to give that challenge a shot before time runs out.

The developing world today can change their destinies if literacy rates are bumped up significantly. That is where the world's community must dare to tread and bring about change. That is how globalism and literacy can change the world.

"Globalisation has brought enormous benefits to humankind, including reduced international poverty, new technologies and shorter distances between countries," the Federal Minister for Europe, Integration and Foreign Affairs of Austria, told the United Nations some years ago.

Sebastian Kurz in his address to the UN General Assembly told his audience: "Events on the other side of the globe can have real impact on our lives. The more the world connects, the more responsibility we have, to not look away from what happens elsewhere and the more we become globalised, the more interest we should have in working for stability and prosperity in other parts of the world," he said.

Well, a greater part of my career as a journalist has been spent researching the factors that keep some countries poor. Then, finally a couple of decades ago, I came to the conclusion that no people in history have remained illiterate and not remained poor. Consequently, I took the view that poorer countries ought to hasten and resolve the chicken and egg question about what comes first in the pursuit to grow their economies. I proposed that it can never be prosperity generated through investments in economic sectors. It's got to be social change that ignites that dream.

Literacy is that elusive link in the economic development chain of Less Developed Countries (LDCs) and the countries that hasten to prepare the climate in which the seed of economic development can germinate - in other words those countries that seek social change through growing literacy - will join the ranks of developed nations. In a nutshell: there can be no development unless men are first educated.

Literacy and poverty are concomitant. The poverty rate falls as literacy levels rise.

Here's an illustration. It demonstrates how with a spike in literacy, poverty levels in India had dropped between 1961 and 2019. In 1961, India's literacy rate hovered at around 40.4 percent according to the Census of India report. At about the same time, economists V. M. Dandekar and Nilakantha Rath, on behalf of the Indian government, estimated that the poverty rate in the 1960s remained generally constant at 41 percent.[1] Notice their concomitance? Then almost six decades later, the National Statistical Commission survey affirmed that India's literacy rate rose to 77.7 percent in 2018,[2] when around the same period, the CIA World Factbook reported India's poverty rate dropped to 21.9 percent of the country's population.[3]

In a brief study I carried out some months ago, I was able to record the literacy and poverty levels of less developed countries in South East Asia and Africa, and I concluded that the concomitance theory of literacy and poverty rings true all the time. In Afghanistan, the literacy level recorded lately stood at

37.3 percent. At about the same time, it's population below the poverty line recorded a level of 54.5 percent. The literacy level down, the poverty level up.[4]

China's adult literacy rate in 2018, on the other hand, was at the top of the ladder's rung at 99.8 percent. With rising literacy levels, its poverty rate fell from an appalling 88 percent in 1981 to 0.7 percent in 2015, as measured by the percentage of people living on the equivalent of US $1.90 or less per day.[5] It now takes second place among the world's biggest economies with a gross domestic product (GDP) of USD $14.72 trillion, second only to the United States of America.[6]

Japan's emergence as an economic juggernaut is an excellent example of how education can jumpstart development. Those who have sought to emulate Japan's resurgence have unfailingly concluded that the most important aspects of the Meiji Restoration were the return of traditional Japanese political systems and the commitment to develop widespread education. The interest in education, which manifested itself in the Tokugawa era, was given fresh impetus in post-war Japan, and these policies hastened the creation of a highly educated workforce which brought about Japan's remarkable economic revival.

Now Japan's impressive literacy rate at 99 percent[7] is credited to be the key to its emergence as an economic juggernaut. It ranks third in the world economy after the US and China with a nominal GDP of $5.06 trillion.[8]

In my earlier book *Can the Poor Inherit the Earth* (2005), I took a closer snapshot at world poverty and the vicious cycle that it inevitably gets trapped in: unbridled population growth, street violence and civil strife, the curse of AIDS or ideologically-driven terrorism. It reviews socialist and capitalist solutions, China's socialist model, India's experiment with capitalism and Africa as a non-starter, despite the international aid pouring in there for decades.

I argue the fact that developing economies cannot rely on the Keynesian theories of GDP growth if the social climate in which the seed of economic prosperity can germinate has not first been prepared. Instead, I make the point that developing economies are required to gradually transform the social, religious, and political institutions which act as obstacles to economic growth.

In other words, I affirm that what is symptomatic of poverty and the vicious cycle is the overwhelming neglect of literacy in developing economies. Literacy is the critical link in the development chain that opens the path to social change.

In a study I was doing some months ago of the state of literacy in our world, what jumped out starkly was the fact that female literacy rates in developing countries are consistently and significantly lower than male literacy. This was particularly true - to name just a few - in Afghanistan, Angola, Bangladesh, Burkina Faso, Benin, Central African Republic, Chad, Pakistan, and Sri Lanka.[9]

It's also estimated that 37 percent of women do not use the internet and 259 million fewer women have access to the Internet than men, even though they account for nearly half the world's population.[10] When you consider the fact that everything today goes through a digital process – whether it's about carrying out a bank transaction or making a medical appointment – you realise our lives depend on modest technological skills, and you begin to see why internet literacy is critical to life.

What equality with men are we talking about? In Afghanistan, Benin, Burkina Faso, Central African Republic, and Chad, female literacy levels range between 18.2 and 37.8 percent.[11] You see, you cannot put an end to a malaise without first peering deep under the carpet. And when you peer deep under the carpet of economic development in poorer countries, you point the finger to illiteracy.

LDCs will be challenged to end violence against women, female infanticide, prenatal sex selection, honor killings, dowry violence, female genital mutilation, marriage by abduction, and forced marriage without first raising female literacy levels in their countries. Why?

That's because you're confronted with a vicious cycle. An illiterate female cannot enter the job market and so contribute to the financial management of the house. She also cannot carry out a bank transaction nor even make a medical appointment because she is computer illiterate. All these man-made impairments have prevented women in developing countries to aspire for an egalitarian society, and women have, as a matter of consequence, acquiesced to be shoved to the backwaters of society in these parts, making them vulnerable to all of the injustices hitherto thrust at them.

If we truly believe that we are one world, one humanity with a common destiny, sharing a common future, we must think globally. The burden otherwise will fall on the shoulders of all humanity, and the common future would be misery. The privileged world has a stake in the ramping up of the economies of the LDCs and perhaps with the leadership of the United Nations, ought to gather together to pave the way for a completely literate planet.

If we go down that road, it is fair to say that a couple of decades from today, the world will see broad-based literate societies unfolding in economically weaker nation states. That will end the frustration of the plebeian masses, the rank and file, and open opportunities in countries across our borders. At that point, migration may no more appear like a haven to citizens of developing countries. Instead, it might seem as if migration would then become an absolutely welcome alternative to propel slowing economies in the West.

Chapter 6

Refugees are Part of our Globalised World

A record 1.3 million migrants applied for asylum in the 28 member states of the European Union, Norway, and Switzerland in 2015 – nearly double the previous high water mark of roughly 700,000 that was set in 1992 after the fall of the Iron Curtain and the collapse of the Soviet Union, according to a PEW Research Center analysis of data from Eurostat, the European Union's statistical agency.[1]

At the end of 2022, 108.4 million people worldwide were forcibly displaced because of persecution, conflict, violence, human rights violations, and events seriously disturbing public order. More than one in every 74 people on Earth has been forced to flee.[2]

Europe was convulsed with this flow of migrants which pushed European states to take divisive positions on the refugee policy, resulting in some closing borders with far-right European political movements promoting distrust of Muslims and white-nationalist conspiracy theorists predicting a Muslim take-over of

Europe. These refugees had arrived in flimsy rubber dinghies and wooden boats on the Greek island of Lesvos, mainly from Syria, Afghanistan, and Iraq.

A humane solution at national borders is achievable.

In the short-term, Europe is already examining strategic programs to humanely confront the migrant crisis. In 2016, the former Secretary General of the United Nations, Ban Ki-moon, was already nudging Europe and the international community to work towards a compassionate and humane solution to the problem – one that respects human rights and complies with international law and grants refugees and migrants the compassion that they are entitled to expect.

"Refugees are only asking what all people deserve: a home, a school and a chance," Mr. Ban said. He credited the UN for offering him global solidarity when he was a six-year-old refugee saying: "without which I would not be standing here."[3]

The UN Special Rapporteur on the Human Rights of Migrants, Francois Crepeau, told the European Union summit in February 2016 that the only way European countries can regain total control of their borders is by creating safe and regular channels for mobility.

"The only way to actually eliminate smuggling is to take over their market by creating regular, safe and cheap mobility solutions with all the identity and security checks that efficient visa procedures can provide," he said.[4]

He was, in fact, asking political leaders in Europe to think outside the box. It's a well-known fact that the forbidden fruit is a temptation, and its prohibition prompts disobedience and revolt. The ability of migrants to reach European soil despite a huge investment in securing international borders has proved that banning entry at the country's borders only serves to empower people traffickers. Long years ago, the Netherlands put marijuana on the free market and in doing so stopped the illegal trade and instead regulated it.

"The European Union must recognize that irregular migration is a result of policies that prohibit immigration," Crepeau said. "Such policies only serve to open new and lucrative markets for smuggling rings, which could not exist without this prohibition. If Europe insists on focussing most of its resources on security, it will fail to defeat smuggling rings," he warned.[5]

He therefore called on the EU to establish a human rights-based coherent and comprehensive migration policy which makes mobility its central asset. "It is the only way in which it can reclaim its border, effectively combat smuggling and empower migrants. Migrants will come, no matter what," Mr. Crepeau warned. The EU will only be able to regain control of its borders if it banks on mobility, he insisted, noting that the overall goal would be to have most migrants using official channels to enter and stay in Europe.

"The EU must develop and create innovative regulated mobility options that will incentivize migrants and asylum seekers to avoid recourse to smugglers," he said. "Instead of forcing people into mechanisms that don't respond to their needs, we need to understand the logic of their decisions and create policies that optimally match migrant's skills and labour market needs."

He enjoined the EU to open more regular migrant channels and at the same time repress unscrupulous employers who exploit the fear of asylum seekers and undocumented migrants of being detected, detained, and deported. "Effectively implementing the employer sanction directive should be a priority," he said. "Combining such policies would lead to smaller, underground labour markets, less irregular border crossings, less smuggling of migrants, less loss of life at borders, less labour exploitation and less migrant's rights violations."

In all of this, what we see is that migrants are being made fair game for verbal and physical abuse feeding off fear and xenophobia. This migrant-bashing should stop, and a meaningful discussion about migrant rights and their integration into mainstream society must begin. In other words, Europe must take back its role as a moral and political leader of human rights in this dismal environment fed with fear and racial prejudice.

In the long term, however, globalism and optimal literacy will ultimately rid the world of the migrant conundrum. Seeking those two noble aspirations will open the world to the brotherhood of man. Tempering the nationalist sentiment with an ideology that embraces the one world, one humanity doctrine, will engender enlightened political leadership and nurture intellectual fodder that feeds the soul with compassion. Globalism and optimal literacy will foster a new morality and create a climate in which tyrants do not germinate and war will be brushed off as a dirty word.

PART III

Create a world with a heart of gold.

Refugees tell their stories of horror: of fleeing from the homeland in the crossfire of war, of witnessing first-hand, the shooting of loved ones, of submitting to torture and shame.

STORY 1

Holocaust survivor tells of the burning of Jews at the crematoriums

"I've seen rows of women stripped naked preparing to be burnt with their children. I've seen daily executions of men and even pregnant women and young girls. I've seen men dig their graves.

I've seen piles and piles of bones in the camps. The Nazis would take us to the pile of bones, make us tie them up with ropes and then burn them."

The late Philip Riteman's prisoner number identification, tattooed on his forearm in the concentration camps of Auschwitz during Hitler's horrifying holocaust, was an everyday reminder to him of what hate can do. "If Hitler was not stopped, there would be no coloured people in the world, and the rest of us would be slaves," he told me. Riteman was commenting on the seriousness of Hitler's resolve to give the world a pure Aryan race.

Riteman was only 13 years old when German soldiers invaded his hometown on the Polish-Russian border and took them to a ghetto teeming with some 35,000 people. Six months later, they were put on trains and taken to Auschwitz. When after a seven-day journey, the train pulled up at Auschwitz station, German soldiers wielding bayonets dispersed the family and, in a flash, Riteman saw his father and mother, five brothers, two sisters, nine uncles and aunts and his grandparents sent to their death.

Riteman was put to hard labour in the Auschwitz, Birkeman, and Dachau camps, building crematoriums where at least 20,000 people were being burnt everyday over day and night shifts. "I've seen rows of women stripped naked preparing to be burnt with their children. I've seen daily executions of men and even pregnant women and young girls. I've seen men dig their graves. I've seen piles and piles of bones in the camps. The Nazis would take us to the pile of bones, make us tie them up with ropes and then burn them."

Riteman, sometimes weeping as he spoke, told of how he was whipped every day while carrying sand and bricks to build those crematoriums. "Fefluckte, they would say and whip us." (Fefluckte is the German word for the "f" expletive). He showed off his crushed thumb that was jammed at the hinge of a door by a German soldier and a bruised neck hit by a flying bullet. He presented photos of bunks at the barracks where he slept on plain board, huddled with other prisoners in those years, and recalled the time when he worked on a farm and lived on oats given to the horses. He said he even survived the "Death March" when prisoners unable to walk anymore were brutally shot by German soldiers.

Riteman finally saw that light at the end of the tunnel four years later one morning. On the horizon he saw soldiers of another kind coming towards the barracks on their stomachs. He looked around and in gaping anticipation realized that the German trucks and tanks had been abandoned. "These were the Americans. They set us free. Our veterans, whether they be Americans, Canadians, or Russians are the only heroes I know," he said.

When the war ended, Riteman lived in a camp where American soldiers and Red Cross personnel were compiling family histories of holocaust survivors. These notes were published in North American newspapers, and that's how two of Riteman's aunts, one in Montreal and the other in Newfoundland, were able to establish contact with him.

The aunt in Montreal failed to convince the government in Ottawa of the need to bring Riteman to Canada. But Newfoundland, which was not part of the Confederation at the time, welcomed him in 1946.

Upon arriving in Canada, Riteman started a rug trading business in Bedford, Nova Scotia, and spent the greater part of his life speaking about the lessons of the holocaust to students at schools, as well as at churches and universities. "I speak for the millions who cannot," he said.

He told me: "I grew up learning never to harm anyone. We believed in the Ten Commandments. But when I came to Auschwitz I said: 'never mind God, where is humanity?"

STORY 2

Mary tells of Chinese people pictured in cartoons eating rats

Mary talks of her encounter with racism as a matter of fact. She says a friend in school once called her home, but her mother who appeared at the door slammed the door shut on her. The following day her friend came crying to her saying she could not play with Mary because she was Chinese. "I was confused. I did not know what was wrong about being Chinese."

Mary Mohammed of *Mary's Bread Basket* fame in Halifax told me some years ago, she looks back on life today and has no regrets. "The world is a beautiful place. I feel free as a bird and life has been good to me." Mary obviously counted her blessings by the flowers that bloom. "Sometimes, unpleasant memories resurrect themselves," she said. "But I quickly dispel them."

Mrs Ling, her mother, was sold to a wealthy Vancouver family by some two old women in China who promised her candy if she came away with them.

Ling later told Mary, her daughter, that she always cried in her early years wanting to know who her family was.

She came to Vancouver when she was barely 11. The host family did not send her to school. Apparently, Mrs Ling did the domestic chores for the Canadian family who got her married, later, to Mr. Ling who came to Canada in 1900 on a cargo ship and paid the mandatory head tax imposed on all Chinese immigrants at the time. The Lings were married in 1918 and came to New Glasgow soon after.

In a long drawn chat at her home in Halifax, Mary told me some poignant stories about growing up Chinese.

"The Chinese bachelors who would visit our home and have meals with us never treated me well. They were good to my brother but caustic in the things they would say to me. They always told me I was no good. The custom was to favour boys who would ultimately become more productive. They excluded me from the Chinese lessons. But my mom loved me dearly and so I grew up a happy child," Mary said.

She said schooling was traumatic, too. "We were not allowed to speak English at home and at school it was only an English-speaking environment and everything felt so foreign to me. I was mortified of the teachers, although they were good to me and assigned a few peers to look after me."

Mary talked of her encounter with racism as a matter of fact. She said a friend in school once called her home, but her mother who appeared at the door slammed the door shut on her. The following day her friend came crying to her saying she could not play with Mary because she was Chinese. "I was confused. I did not know what was wrong about being Chinese. Apparently, we were thought to be the world's scary creatures pictured in cartoons with pigtails, slanted eyes and eating rats."

The fact of being Chinese, she said, was something that she was reminded of again and again. "When I was interviewed for a job at a store, the manager tried to fondle me and I resisted that. I was later told I could not get the job because I was Chinese." Mary says she felt the same discrimination when a property developer hesitated to sell her a plot, not sure if the neighbors would approve of them.

But looking back, Mary liked to laugh at some of the other events in her life. Her father was once taken to court, she told me, for possession of a tonic. "The police were looking for opium in our house and when they found this clay pot, they broke it up and the potion fell to the floor. Assuming this was opium, father was dragged to court," she said, laughing out loud. She told me that was Chinese tonic, made from white-tipped deer tails, several snakes, Chinese herbs, red dates, seal penis, gin, hop and pieces of crow.

In 1955, Mary got married to the late Mo Mohammed, a scientist at the Naval Research Department, where she worked as well. Mo was a Trinidadian of Indian descent. Together, they had three boys and a girl.

Although Mary acknowledged that her values of honesty and hard work were akin to the values of any Canadian, she said she felt very Chinese and was very Chinese at heart. "Unfortunately, when I married Mo, the Chinese people were prejudiced and ostracized my family, saying I was a disgrace to the Chinese."

Mary's "Bread Basket," for which she is famous, was opened in 1983. But she realizes that man does not live on bread alone. She said she lived on every ounce of joy that life brought her.

STORY 3

Canadian patient screams at the sight of Nigerian doctor

The experience with his very first patient, Mrs Phillips, was an unforgettable one.

"I was assigned to provide her with breathing exercises and vasodilation," Dr. Eni told me. "But at my very sight, the lady screamed and yelled so loudly that the nurses rushed to her bedside. I was very disturbed to know later that she had never seen a Black man, having been raised in a rural town on the Manitoba-Saskatchewan border."

When the three-year long Nigeria-Biafra war was coming to an end, there was enormous suffering among the defeated Ibo population of Eastern Nigeria. The country was ruled by military dictatorship at the time and foreign travel was, naturally, restricted, especially for the elitists and those who fought on the Biafran side. There were military roadblocks at every major highway, and many of the Ibos living outside of their homeland were in hiding.

Dr. Godwin Eni, an Ibo, was discreet about his movements but was fortunate to have some protection from two prominent non-Ibo professors at the University of Ibadan as well as a policewoman. He says he was the first Nigerian physiotherapist trained at the University of Ibadan, and his professors, therefore, appeared to feel somewhat of an obligation to protect him.

The political environment was tense. The military governed the four regions of Nigeria. There was severe devastation in the Biafran region. The properties of many Ibos in the non-Ibo regions of Nigeria were confiscated or appropriated by the military. The Biafran currency was banned by the military, thereby rendering the region unsustainable economically.

Dr. Eni was on the blacklist of professionals and was barred from travelling abroad. And to compound things, there were roadblocks on major highways, rampant harassment of the population by soldiers, and many instances of brutality. "But I decided I had to flee Nigeria," he said. "The two professors from the university of Ibadan made it possible. They pulled their weight to obtain my Nigerian passport and smuggle me through the Ikeja airport enroute to

London, England. The passenger airplane was delayed at the tarmac in order to get me on board."

Dr. Eni arrived in Montreal on October 6, 1970, with a bullet lodged in his armpit and 50 Pounds Sterling in his pocket. It was the time when the FLQ, the terrorist group, had kidnapped the British Trade Commissioner in Montreal, and the mood outside the airport was tense with military tanks on alert. Anyway, three days later he arrived in Saskatoon and took up assignment at the University Hospital.

The experience with his very first patient, Mrs Phillips, was an unforgettable one.

"I was assigned to provide her with breathing exercises and vasodilation," Dr. Eni told me. "But at my very sight, the lady screamed and yelled so loudly that the nurses rushed to her bedside. I was very disturbed to know later that she had never seen a Black man, having been raised in a rural town on the Manitoba-Saskatchewan border."

Dr. Eni says he felt humiliated and inferior. He told the Head of Rehabilitation Medicine that he was returning to Nigeria.

He told me he could have, professionally, been very successful in Nigeria, but not as a member of the Ibo tribe at that time. He had suffered arrest and indignities as an Ibo living and working in a non-Ibo region of the country. When in hiding, he lived in fear for his life. He had a handsome job as a physiotherapist at the University Hospital in Ibadan. But the constant fear for his safety coupled with the fact that he did not speak the language of the region kept him in jeopardy.

Nonetheless, he returned to Nigeria in 1972 as a lecturer at the University of Ife in Western Nigeria.

"I was glad to return to Nigeria having endured cultural isolation in cold Saskatoon. I thought that the country had progressed politically and that some degree of order and stability had returned to the regions. But I quickly realized that my expectations were premature. The country's soldiers were traumatising people of the Eastern region. I could not travel freely even to my home region without considerable fear for my safety. There were more police and military roadblocks on every major road. I had regular nightmares. As a result, and under those conditions, I returned to Canada."

"This time there were no shocking episodes of discrimination at the hospital," he said. "None like the experience with Ms Philips." Nonetheless, prejudice was evident.

He told me of a time when an apartment for rent was suddenly rented out when he showed up as a potential tenant. The same apartment became available one hour later when his Caucasian wife enquired about a vacancy.

On another day, a student, not aware that he was the director of graduate studies and Chair of the admissions committee at the university, uttered a racist slur to a fellow student in his presence and spoke about the need to limit the enrolment of immigrant communities in the program and faculty. In his conversation, he implied that Blacks, Chinese, and other Asian applicants were not sufficiently "Canadian" and rational enough to assimilate the knowledge and rigor associated with graduate studies in health services, planning, and administration. He was astonished to meet Dr. Eni as Program Director later in the day.

But putting aside these memories, Dr. Eni says, he is today proud of his two nationalities: Nigerian and Canadian. "The former gives me a cultural base and a certain sense of self that provides me with a unique identity and cultural appreciation in a multicultural environment. The latter provides me with a unique sense of belonging to the best country in the world where all cultures meet and live together in harmony, peacefully and in safety."

STORY 4

Cambodian baby flown to Canada in the heat of the war

Her flight out of Cambodia a month later was like what one sees in the movies. As buildings crumbled, corpses piled up, and shrapnel flew dangerously across the orphanage, Bopha and the other abandoned babies were driven to the airport. They were huddled in a truck that was draped with the Red Cross insignia to escape the vigilant eye of the Khmer Rouge patrols. She flew to Saigon and stayed there for some weeks until a "baby lift" of Indo-Chinese orphans brought her to Canada.

Sue-San Bopha's narration of the story of her life will remind many of the Old Testament story: The woman, fearing for her son's life, tip-toed to the river with her son Moses in a basket and lowered the child into the water. Then she watched it sail away as she prayed for his safety.

Bopha was born in Cambodia during the heat of the war in 1975 when the invading Khmer Rouge was bombing and devastating the city of Phnom Penh. During the purges of the next four years, one in four Cambodians were sent to the notorious Killing Fields, and Bopha could have been one of them.

She was only two weeks old at the time, when amid gunfire and explosions, two caring hands of someone anonymous placed her at the doorstep of a Phnom Penh orphanage called *Canada House* and left. Along with 43 other children, Bopha was adopted by the orphanage. Canada House is just one of the orphanages under the umbrella of "Families for Children," a private adoption agency in Ontario with orphanages in several parts of the developing world.

Her flight out of Cambodia a month later was like what one sees in the movies. As buildings crumbled, corpses piled up, and shrapnel flew dangerously across the orphanage, Bopha and the other abandoned babies were driven to the airport. They were huddled in a truck that was draped with the Red Cross insignia to escape the vigilant eye of the Khmer Rouge patrols. She flew to Saigon and stayed there for some weeks until a "baby lift" of Indo-Chinese orphans brought her to Canada, to the home of Gwen and George King in Edmonton, who raised her with love and affection.

The story would never have been told but for an emotional reunion in Montreal twenty six summers later that brought together Sue-San King and the other "grown babies" to meet with sisters Dolly and Anna Charet and Naomi Bronstein who had sheltered the abandoned children in Cambodia during the war.

King moved to Halifax from Edmonton many years ago after graduating in modern languages (German and French) at the University of Lethbridge in Alberta. She worked as a Research Assistant for the Robertson Surette Group at the time.

King is not bitter about her past. "Although my background hadn't created a sense of curiosity in my teens, I now have the urge to know my roots," she told me. "I don't even know if there is one person in my bloodline in Cambodia today. But if I go, it will not be a search for my people....I just want to smell and feel the land I belong to."

She said that if she goes, she may even consider staying back. "I have a deep concern for Cambodian issues, not necessarily Cambodians, and want to work with war-affected children."

King told me: "The reunion in Montreal was an emotional one, not because I met with Cambodians with a similar fate as mine, but because I met with the people that cared for me." She said she had an emotional one-to-one with sisters Dolly and Anna and with Bronstein. "But as Cambodians, we hardly sat down and shared notes. People think there will be commonalities to share when people of like races meet. But that's not necessarily how it is."

Anyone would think that orphans lack a mother's love. But King refutes that. "I've not felt that lack. I've been given all of it by Gwen and George. It doesn't matter, who gives it to you."

King is also an accomplished singer. Many years ago, she travelled extensively to the United States and Europe with the group "Up with People" singing songs about poverty, racism, and justice issues. "That was a hands-on experience with global citizenship," she told me. "I've had a good time in my life. I'm proud of this progress and this journey."

And somewhere in the world, those caring hands of someone anonymous that placed a baby on the steps of Canada House decades ago must be proud, too.

STORY 5

Kosovar doctor recalls the nightmare of war

"Tanks were parked outside my house in Pristina. The soldiers were burning houses and shooting in the streets. NATO planes were bombing through the night. We escaped to a friend's house at safe distance from the tanks. But that was momentary comfort. That night the police officers nabbed us and ordered us out of our homes. They yelled at us, kicked the others and asked for gold and cash.

When the war in Kosovo got ugly and Dr. Luli Rrafshi's wife was nine months pregnant, he had cut short his Residency at Bucharest to be with her at this critical time. Then seven days after the NATO strikes began, the Serb forces began a brutal expulsion of Albanians.

"Tanks were parked outside my house in Pristina. The soldiers were burning houses and shooting in the streets. NATO planes were bombing through the night. We escaped to a friend's house at safe distance from the tanks. But that was momentary comfort," he told me.

Rrafshi says that night the police officers nabbed them and ordered them out of their homes. "They yelled at us, kicked the others and asked for gold and cash."

He tells an interesting tale here. He says he gave away the keys of his car and some cash. But they asked for more. So, he proffered his wedding ring. The constable looked at it and said he wouldn't take that because wedding rings are sacred. Luli thought to himself: "Here's a criminal afraid of God."

Along with some 10,000 other Albanians, Rrafshi and his wife were being expelled that night. He remembers the silent march to nowhere. Many thought they were being taken to the killing fields. He says Albanians were beaten with rifles on the way and were finally put on buses and trains and moved to the Macedonian border where many died.

Rrafshi was lucky. UN personnel fought their way with Macedonian officials at the border and got him and his wife into a camp; three nights later, she delivered a baby girl at a hospital. He then went shopping for refugee status in the tents where American, Australian, and Canadian immigration officials were interviewing refugees. He turned to the Canadians and the following morning saw his name on the list of those approved to fly to Canada.

The war may be over. But the scars remain. Some years after the war, he travelled to Kosovo with Canadian friends. "The people had changed. So many were still in a state of trauma, hopelessness, many without their homes, their relationships were cold. And there were minefields everywhere," he said.

Rrafshi believes it's going to be very hard for Serbs and Albanians to be friends again. War has taught everyone that it achieves nothing. It only destroys. The wounds will take a lifetime to heal. He remembers stories told to him in the camp: The story about the old man with four women and lots of kids who said he was living to protect his daughters-in-law, after his four sons were killed in his presence. He recalls the story of the family that was leaving home in their tractor and was stopped by soldiers who dragged their daughters away and shot the son, leaving the father to bury him.

Rrafshi's father, who now lives with his daughter in London, was almost killed during the war – beaten brutally with a knife at his throat.

STORY 6

Vietnamese chooses dangerous sea ordeal to flee.

Nguyen says there were Thai pirates out there at sea, waiting to attack boat passengers and take their possessions. "We were attacked seven times. These guys in boats were encircling our boat. They flashed their guns, ripped up pieces of baggage and took away their spoils."

When the communists took power in Vietnam in 1975, boats crammed with fleeing Vietnamese were taking off routinely, and Terry Nguyen's father chose to jump on one of them in August 1979. At the time, there were Chinese agents faking identity papers, so the Nguyens filed their papers as Chinese residents whose departure from Vietnam was, in fact, facilitated by the Vietnamese government.

Nguyen and the family were taking a boat to Malaysia, but the road to the island where a boat could be boarded was monitored. "We could have been caught and jailed," said Terry Nguyen, who was about twenty years at the time. "This was a 24-metre boat on which 523 Vietnamese were fleeing. Then it got worse once we were in international waters."

Nguyen says there were Thai pirates out there at sea, waiting to attack boat passengers and take their possessions. "We were attacked seven times. These guys in boats were encircling our boat. They flashed their guns, ripped up pieces of baggage and took away their spoils. When they had finished, another group of pirates would come along."

The last batch of pirates finally stole their boat engine. "We kept floating in the middle of the sea. We looked for birds for the comfort of knowing we were close to shore, but there were none."

The Nguyens were at sea for five days, and on the last couple of days lived without food or water. "Ironically, the last group of pirates who saw we were desperate and with no possessions, threw us some food from their boats." Eventually, this boat was rescued by a German ship.

Looking back, Nguyen says "Freedom is not free. That's what we had to trade for freedom." In a refugee camp in Malaysia, a Canadian officer convinced the Nguyens that Canada was a better destination than the United States. So, the family settled in Truro in the province of Nova Scotia, beginning a new life in a new world. "In Truro, we would cycle to work, but kids out of curiosity would cycle alongside us and some of them would bully us. We ignored that."

Nguyen believes the times are changing but even today when things go wrong, racism surfaces. "I've heard people say the Vietnamese grow pot and become prosperous. That denigrates an entire society. That's incorrect."

In Halifax, he did a few semesters in engineering at Saint Mary's University and later got married and at the time took up a job as a computer analyst. But he remembers the hard times even in Canada. "At a point in time, I delivered pizza, drove a taxi and washed dishes in three different jobs in order to pay back my student loans and feed the family."

That, indeed, is the enigma of arrival!

STORY 7

Somalian hopes Canada will erase those horror memories

Hadil's child was nine days old when a gang of looters broke into her house and seized her husband. "They wanted all our money and my jewellery," she said. "I said I would give anything for my husband's life. But they shot him in the head, buried him in the backyard and left."

Hadil Hassan, who was in the deadly midst of it all during the civil war in Somalia, is hoping that life in Canada shall someday erase those memories.

Hadil's child was nine days old when a gang of looters broke into her house and seized her husband. "They wanted all our money and my jewellery," she said. "I said I would give anything for my husband's life. But they shot him in the head, buried him in the backyard and left."

A couple of days later, Hadil's father's house was blown up, and as the bloody civil war penetrated the neighbouring villages, Hadil's family chose to flee.

Her husband's people fled to Kenya, and Hadil's family began the long journey across the border to Ethiopia.

"The war was traumatic," she told me. "Every couple of steps along the way we saw blood and death, children maimed." The journey to Ethiopia took a couple of months. She even lost her mother along the way, thankfully for only a couple of days. In Ethiopia, they lived on wheat brought to the refugee camps by the Red Cross.

But war also has a way of tearing people apart. So, when a couple of years later, her father proposed that she marry her husband's brother, she travelled to Kenya with him, leaving her son behind with her mother. Hadil's second husband was a translator at the Canadian mission in Kenya, and that obviously made the Canadian connection. The Hassans travelled to Canada. But the trials were far from over.

When Hadil's father returned home to Somalia with her son, he was assassinated. The boy's early years were a witness to the ugliness of Somalia's civil war.

But Hadil knew deep inside her that the reunion with her son in Canada would someday bring a new dawn.

STORY 8

Journalist once hobnobbing with Saddam Hussein flees Iraq

Lami was walking a tight rope and in early 1998 played into Hussein's hands with an editorial titled: "Freedom of Hell". The Iraqi leader was outraged and ordered his imprisonment.

When in the wee hours of January 16, 1991, the United States and its allies began the bombing of Baghdad in Iraq, the world woke up to the reality of a war being fought by one man against the might of 27 nations of the world. That man was Saddam Hussein, the protagonist in the Gulf War and who was later hanged for the crimes against his people.

Sabah Al Lami, at the time, editor-in-chief of *Al Mustaqba* (*The Future*) had been hobnobbing with the Iraqi leader in the post-Gulf war years and was counted among the elite in the media, a front-row journalist at news conferences in the Presidential Palace. In those years, Lami was cautiously speaking out against injustices and human rights abuses witnessed in Iraq. "I did this discreetly, never confronting the President directly, but pointing some questions in his direction," he told me.

But apparently Lami was walking a tight rope and in early 1998 played into Hussein's hands with an editorial titled: *Freedom of Hell*. The Iraqi leader was outraged and ordered his imprisonment along with other eminent journalists in Baghdad at the time. Lami was sent to Al Radhwaniah jail. He told me the experience was like being thrown among lions where prisoner beatings were commonplace.

The jail term served as reflection time for Lami, whose book *Maqalad azajad Saddam Hussein* took shape then. The title translated in English reads: *The stories that enraged Saddam Hussein*.

When he had done his six-month term at Al Radhwaniah, Lami was put under house arrest, and the President's office ordered his name to be blacklisted at Iraq's border exits. But he was determined to flee the repression. "There's nothing money cannot buy in Iraq today," he said. He bribed a passport department official with about US $1,000, who discreetly erased his name on the blacklist, issued him a new passport in the name given at birth, by which he was not known, and on November 6, 1998, he crossed Iraq's border into Jordan.

In the following months, Lami hired lawyers to change family records, declare his wife dead and register a new name. Once again, he forked out some US $5,000 to a passport department official to ease the way out of Iraq for his wife and six sons. He told me his other colleagues under house arrest who preferred not to pay their way out of Iraq were rearrested at the border points from where they attempted to flee and were thrown again into jails.

Lami and his family spent the next two years in Jordan where he wrote prolifically for the London-based Arab magazine *Al Zaman* and published his book *Maqalad azajad Saddam Hussein*. At the same time, Lami also applied to the United Nations High Commission for Refugees (UNHCR), seeking refugee status. Two years later, he was welcomed by the Canadian government.

His book is a narrative on the human rights abuses and injustices witnessed in Iraq back in the day. One of them is a story of the displacement of some 500 Shia families who had moved to Baghdad from Southern Iraq just prior to the Gulf War.

"Hussein's government organized the complete demolition of these 500 villas by tractors," Lami told me. "The civil conflict that erupted after the Gulf War was a reflection of how much Hussein felt threatened by the Shias of Iraq – an Islamic sect opposed to the ruling Sunni government."

Lami, who was present at most of Hussein's Press briefings at the Palace prior to the bombing of Baghdad, said the Iraqi leader was absolutely aware that the war would devastate Iraq but decided to take his country to that brink.

"The oil embargo on Iraq was not an evil act of the United Nations or of the United States," he said. "Hussein was the real killer of those children who were dying without food or medicine."

STORY 9

Kurdish farmer escapes Iraq's chemical poisoning.

Haaji, a Kurdish farmer from Shimaal in the north of Iraq, woke up terrorized one morning having learnt that some 5,000 people in the neighbouring villages of Halabjah were killed in a chemical poison attack ordered by Iraqi President Saddam Hussein in 1988. That day Haaji saw some 40,000 Kurds, like an ocean of humanity, making a silent exodus out of Iraq and a forced entry into Turkey.

It would seem natural to expect that settling down in another country, hit by the culture shock of white faces and foreign custom, would be a cakewalk for anyone who has eluded the watchful eye of a secret service agency or fled in the face of a chemical poison attack. But that's not quite true. That's the painful dilemma of transition for some newcomers to Canada.

Haaji, a Kurdish farmer from Shimaal in the north of Iraq, woke up terrorized one morning having learnt that some 5,000 people in the neighbouring villages of Halabjah were killed in a chemical poison attack ordered by Iraqi President Saddam Hussein in 1988. That day Haaji saw some 40,000 Kurds, like an ocean of humanity, making a silent exodus out of Iraq and a forced entry into Turkey.

"It was impossible to stay back. Saddam's army was shooting men and taking their wives and children away to be left at camps," he said. "I ordered my mother, wife and nine children to rise and leave."

In the dead of night, Haaji got his mother and three children to mount a pony, while he led the rest of the family on the two-day long trek on foot to the borders of Turkey.

The active Kurdish resistance in Iraq had begun in the early eighties which ultimately forced Saddam's army to get brutal. The Kurds, who have been fighting for a homeland, have been scattered across Southern Turkey, Northern Iraq, Syria, and Iran.

Haaji's exodus was like an unending saga of trials and tribulation. His daughter was lost in the melee one night, forcing him to make a sinuous retreat. On his way back, he lost his mother, but was reunited again at the Turkish border. They continued the trek only through the night and hid in the caves of surrounding hills in the day to avoid being seen by Iraqi soldiers. His cousin's wife, on the journey, who was about to deliver a baby, was confronted with the fact that her 18-month-old child in arms was about to die. "One moment she was burying a child, another moment she was giving birth to one," he told me. But fleeing has its quota of troubles, and Haaji's troubles were not any different.

Upon approaching Turkey's border, Haaji got to know that Turkish soldiers were actually handing Kurdish refugees back to Iraqi forces. But he took heart and with help from United Nations peacekeepers was brought under UN protection and accommodated in a refugee camp on Turkey's border.

Haaji lived in those refugee camps for four years. "It was like hell. People were dying for the lack of food and blankets. Turkish soldiers were poisoning the bread that was being distributed to Kurdish refugees. There was no work," he said. Then, four years later, consular staff from Germany, the United States, and Canada got there and extricated refugees from their plight granting them refugee status under the Convention Refugee Act.

By 1992, the family was welcomed into Canada along with 300 other Kurdish families. But the early years in Canada were not a bed of roses. The clash of civilizations tore the family apart. His eldest daughter left home. "She abandoned our sense of discipline and walked out," he said. His wife explained: "She's under the care of Children's Aid and we are not allowed to see her. This, in itself, is hell. Nobody is even trying to bring us together."

Haaji has the creature comforts that Canadians desire to be happy. But he is not. There is a sense that you can flee from hell on the ground, but you cannot easily flee from hell in the mind.

Epilogue

The epilogue in my previous book *Global Healing* presents the view that optimal literacy on the planet will ultimately pave the path to a peaceable world. In it, I contend that a well-rounded education is key to the challenge of change. Academic literacy eliminates poverty by engaging societies in economic development. It moderates migration and the movement of people outside their national borders because in literate societies, the jobs are in the home country. It scorns race-driven prejudice and dispels ignorance which is the foundation of race-driven hate. Likewise, moral literacy creates a society that abhors violence and the scourge of war and creates the climate in which nations are transformed and driven to spawn and engender peaceable generations. Moral education, I said, fosters national morality.

This book, which is a serial to that title, broadens that view. It presents the setting of a stage in which people of the world would seek to live and develop their economies as one humanity. Globalization is not optional. The wisdom in *Ubuntu* is this: "I am because we are." How can one be at peace when others around you are in misery? The history of conflict on the planet is a narrative of how the marginalized, the plebeian, rank and file masses have turned against the bourgeoisie – our capitalist societies.

The marginalized, the plebeian, rank and file masses must sit with us all at the same table, and peace will be within grasp. The extreme right-wing nationalist may be opposed to this notion and, indeed, all of us have a right to hold the views we choose.

But globalism is an opportunity for two worlds apart to come together for the common good, to share common responsibility for a common future. If we choose not to, it really boils down to this: Either we live together or we die together.

References

Chapter 1
The Troubles with Nationalism

1. "World Nuclear Forces, SIPRI yearbook 2020". *Stockholm International Peace Research Institute*. January 2020. Wikipedia: <https://en.wikipedia.org/wiki/List_of_states_with_nuclear_weapons>.

2. Stockholm International Peace Research Institute (SIPRI) <https://www.sipri.org/media/pressreleases>

3. Ibid.

4. Ibid.

5. Ibid.

6. United Nations: https://news.un.org/en/story/2018/09/1020472

7. Media Reports

8. Brexit: https://en.wikipedia.org/wiki/Causes_of_the_vote_in_favour_of_Brexit

9. Anders Behring Breivik <https://en.wikipedia.org/wiki/Anders_Behring_Breivik>

10. Media Reports

11. Ibid.

12. Ibid.

13. UN Dispatch: <http://undispatch.com/un-high-commissioner-human-rights-just-job/>

Chapter 2
Globalism is Not an Option

1. "World Exports as Percentage of Gross World Product". Global Policy Forum. Archived from the original on 12 July 2008. <https://en.wikipedia.org/wiki/History_of_globalization>

2. Canada.ca https://www.canada.ca/en/immigration-refugees-citizenship/news/2022/12/canada-welcomes-historic-number-of-newcomers-in-2022.html

Chapter 3
Migration is a Catalyst

1. Saggi, Kamal (2002). "Trade, Foreign Direct Investment, and International Technology Transfer: A Survey". *World Bank Research Observer.* 17 (2): 191235. CiteSeerX 10.1.1.17.7732. doi:10.1093/wbro/17.2.191. S2CID 16620922. https://en.wikipedia.org/wiki/Globalization

2. Government of Canada. https://www.international.gc.ca/trade-commerce/trade-agreements-accords-commerciaux/agr-acc/nafta-alena/fta-ale/facts.aspx?lang=eng

3. Asia Pacific Economic Cooperation (APEC) https://www.apec.org/about-us/about-apec/achievements-and-benefits#:~:text=Its%2021%20member%20

economies%20are,USD%2046.9%20trillion%20in%20-2018.

4. Sohail Inayatullah is an Australian academic and a Professor at the Graduate Institute of Futures Studies at Tamkang University in Taipei, Taiwan.

5. Dr. Howard Duncan, Chair Emeritus, International Metropolis Project and former Editor of *International Migration.*

Chapter 4
Religious Diversity is a Boon, Not a Threat

1. Media Reports
2. Ibid.
3. Ibid.
4. Canada.ca <https://www.canada.ca/en/immigration-refugees-citizenship/news/2022/12/canada-welcomes-historic-number-of-newcomers-in-2022.html>
5. IRCC: Canada welcomes the most immigrants in a single year in its history, 23 December 2021. https://www.canada.ca/en/immigration-refugees-citizenship/news/2021/12/canada-welcomes-the-most-immigrants-in-a-single-year-in-its-history.html.

Chapter 5
Literacy is Key to its Success

1.. Dandekar and Rath: "Poverty in India" Economic and Political Weekly, 6 (2) 9 January 1971. Retrieved 16 August 2017.

2. National Statistical Commission, NSO 2018, P.1.

3. CIA World Factbook https://www.cia.gov/the-world-factbook/countries/india/

4. CIA World Factbook https://www.cia.gov/the-world-factbook/countries/afghanistan/

5. "Overview," Worldbank.org.

6. World Bank

7. Organization for Economic Cooperation and Development (OECD) PISA

8. World Bank

9. CIA World Factbook

10. United Nations

11. CIA World Factbook

Chapter 6
Refugees are Part of our Globalised World

1. pewresearch.org/global/2016/08/02/Pew Research Center, Washington, D.C. (August 2, 2016)

2. UNHCR: Global Trends: Forced Displacement in 2020 <https://www.unhcr.org/global-trends>

3. UNHCR: < https://www.unhcr.org/news/news/un-secretary-general-receives-unhcr-withrefugees-petition>

4 United Nations < https://www.ohchr.org/en/press-releases/2016/03/eu-migration-summit-some-european-states-showing-complete-disregard-human#:~:text=The%20only%20way%20for%20Europe,more%20risky%20journeys%20with%20smugglers

5. Ibid.

www.ingramcontent.com/pod-product-compliance
Lightning Source LLC
LaVergne TN
LVHW020934090426
835512LV00020B/3351